AF601971

For Fred Ehrlich, M.D.,
in appreciation for his careful
review of the text and art

CIP data is available.

Published in the United States 2013 by
Blue Apple Books
South Orange, New Jersey
www.blueapplebooks.com

You Can't See Your BONES WITH BINOCULARS!

Harriet Ziefert • pictures by Amanda Haley

You can't see your bones with binoculars, but a radiologist can surely see them on X-ray.

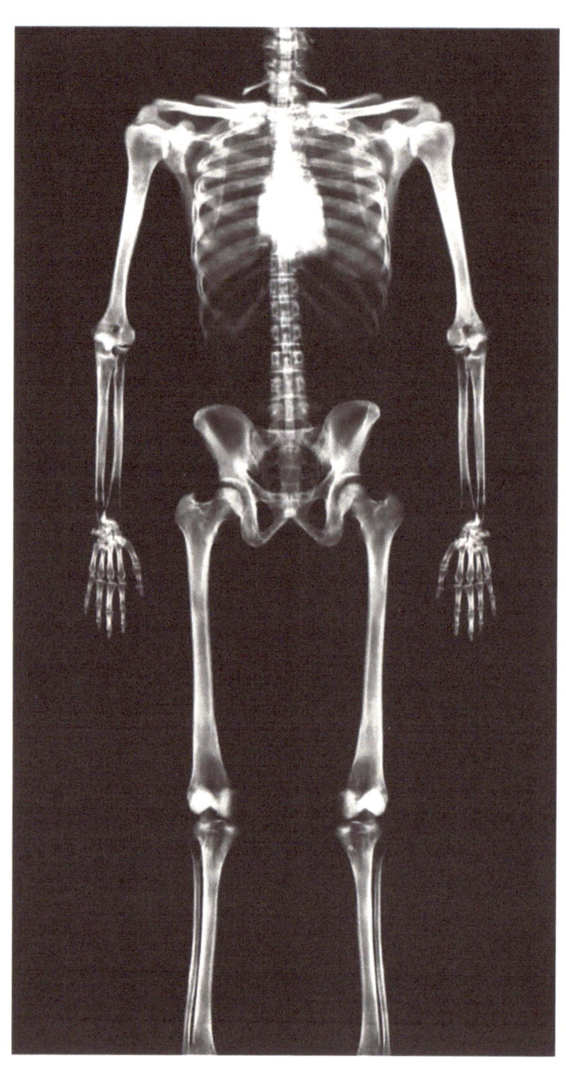

Babies have about 450 bones at birth, but by the time they are your age, they only have 206. Why? Because many bones, like those in the skull, grow together.

Come on a guided tour of the bones in your body... look at the X-rays, but also make sure to stop and run your hand along the bone or bones being described.

The head bone is connected to the neck bones.

Put your hands around your head and push. Hard, isn't it? That's because your brain needs to be protected, and the bones in your skull do quite a good job.

If your skull were soft like a ripe cantaloupe, your brain could get mushed and then you would have a very bad day!

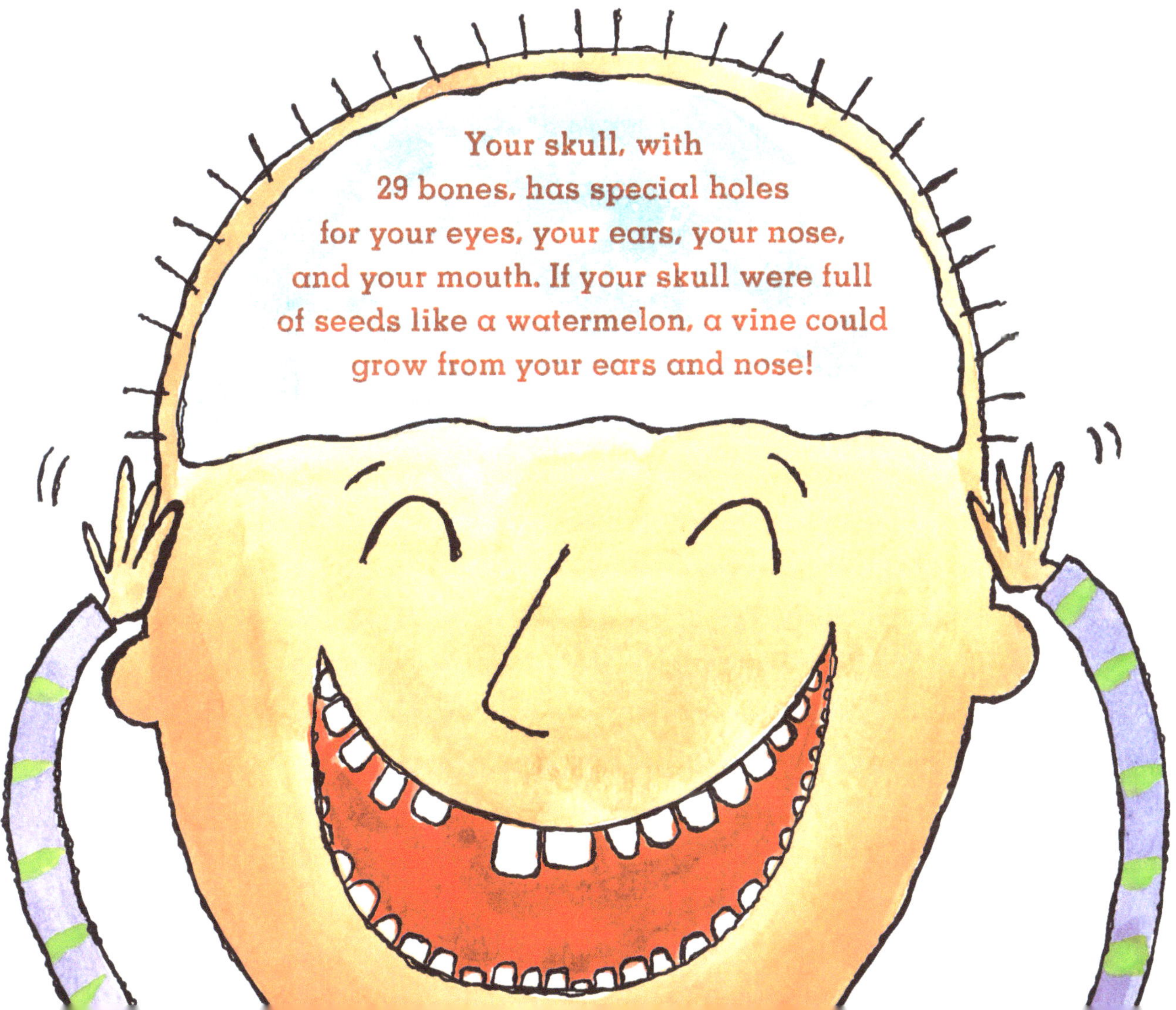

The neck  bones are connected

Put your fingers on the back of your neck. The hard things you feel are your neck bones, also known as cervical vertebrae.

Each vertebra has a  hole in the middle for the spinal cord to go through.

Turn your head
from side to side

up
and and
down.

The bones move!

to the shoulder bones.

The topmost neck bone holds up your head. (No, not your cantaloupe, Charlie!) It is called the atlas and is named after the giant who holds the world on his shoulders in a Greek story.

The shoulder bones are connected

Put your hand on your shoulder and move your arm around. If it feels complicated, you're right! The shoulder is very complicated.

Bones called the clavicle and the scapula come together to form a socket. The "ball" at the top of another bone called the humerus rotates so that you can move your arm in all directions.

to the back bones.

Pitchers have trouble with their rotator cuffs, which are muscles that hold the shoulder together. This trouble is because nobody told the muscles they were supposed to throw baseballs at 100 miles per hour!

The back  bones are connected

It's hard to feel your own backbone, but it's quite easy to move your fingers down someone else's. The bumps you feel are vertebrae (not walnuts, unless you have a really weird mind). It will be hard to feel all 24 of them, but it's worth a try.

Just as the skull protects your brain, the main task of the backbone is to protect your spinal cord.

to the hip bone.

The hip bone is connected

Start at your neck and move your fingers down your chest. Your ribs are bones that move when you breathe. You have 12 pairs of them, and they make a cage. Is there a canary inside? No, there are two lungs and a heart in the middle.

You'll soon arrive at your belly—the big, squishy place where your liver, spleen, intestines, stomach, and other terrific things hang out. None of these are bony!

to the thigh bone.

The first hard thing you hit below your belly is your hip bone, or pelvis, which is made up of six bones. The rounded, hard point that pokes out on each side is the anterior superior iliac crest. If you use this word at the dinner table, everyone will be impressed, but do not try to say it with your mouth full of food!

The thigh bone is connected

The thigh bone is the biggest and heaviest bone you have.

to the knee bone.

It's hard to feel your thigh bone, or femur, because it's covered by big muscles, which you need for walking,

jumping,

and running away from alligators!

The knee bone is connected

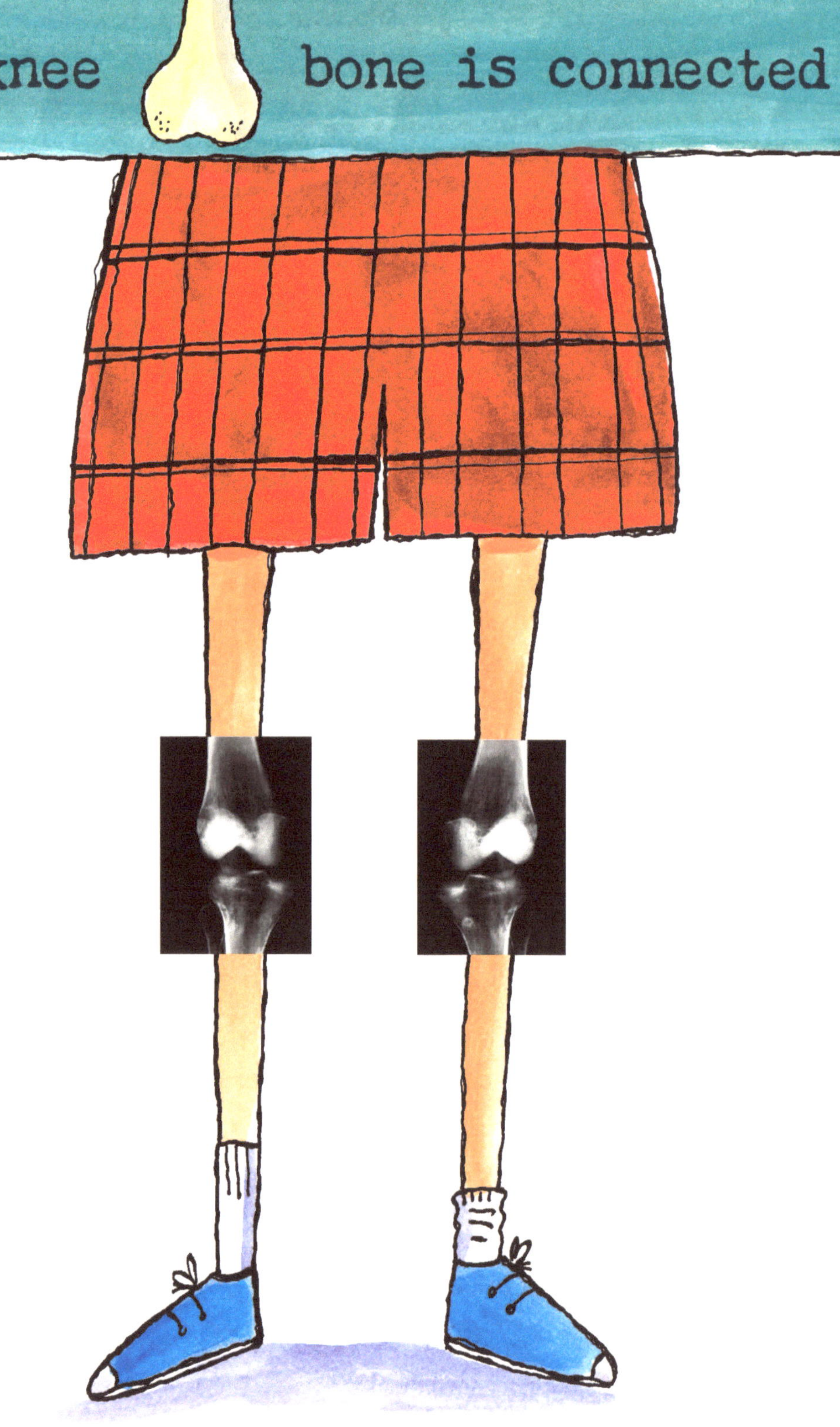

Kneel on a hard floor. After a while, your kneecaps, or patellas, will probably start to hurt because there's only skin and not much padding on them.

to the leg bones.

All of these people use different kinds of knee pads to protect their knees. If you're going to sneak out of the house on your hands and knees, be sure to wear knee pads!

football players,

gardeners,

hockey goalies,

carpenters.

The leg  bones are connected

There are actually two bones in the lower leg,

the tibia and the fibula.

You can feel the tibia at the front of your lower leg. It's the shin bone that hurts a whole lot when your little brother kicks you.

The fibula is on the little toe side of your leg and is harder to feel because it's much smaller.

But give it a try anyway.

to the ankle bones.

The ankle  bones are connected

The protrusions (it never hurts to learn a new word) that people think are their ankles are really part of the leg bones. The ankle bones are hidden away where you can't really feel them.

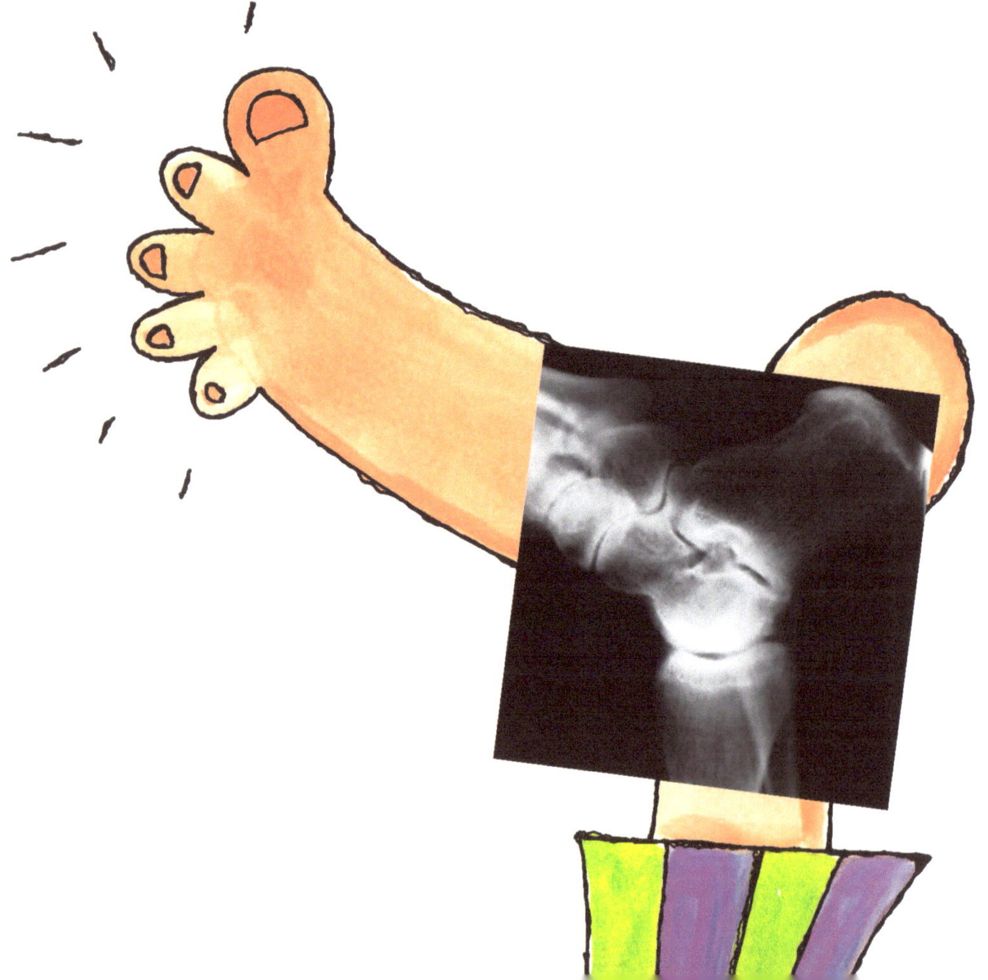

to the foot bones.

They do, however, have neat names like "navicular," and "calcaneus," and "cuneiform." But if you tell your friends you know all this, they will think you are terribly nerdy and won't talk to you for a week.

The foot bones are connected

There are 26 bones in your foot–metatarsals on the flat, front part and phalanges in the toes. Because your foot is so bony, you can probably feel a lot of them.

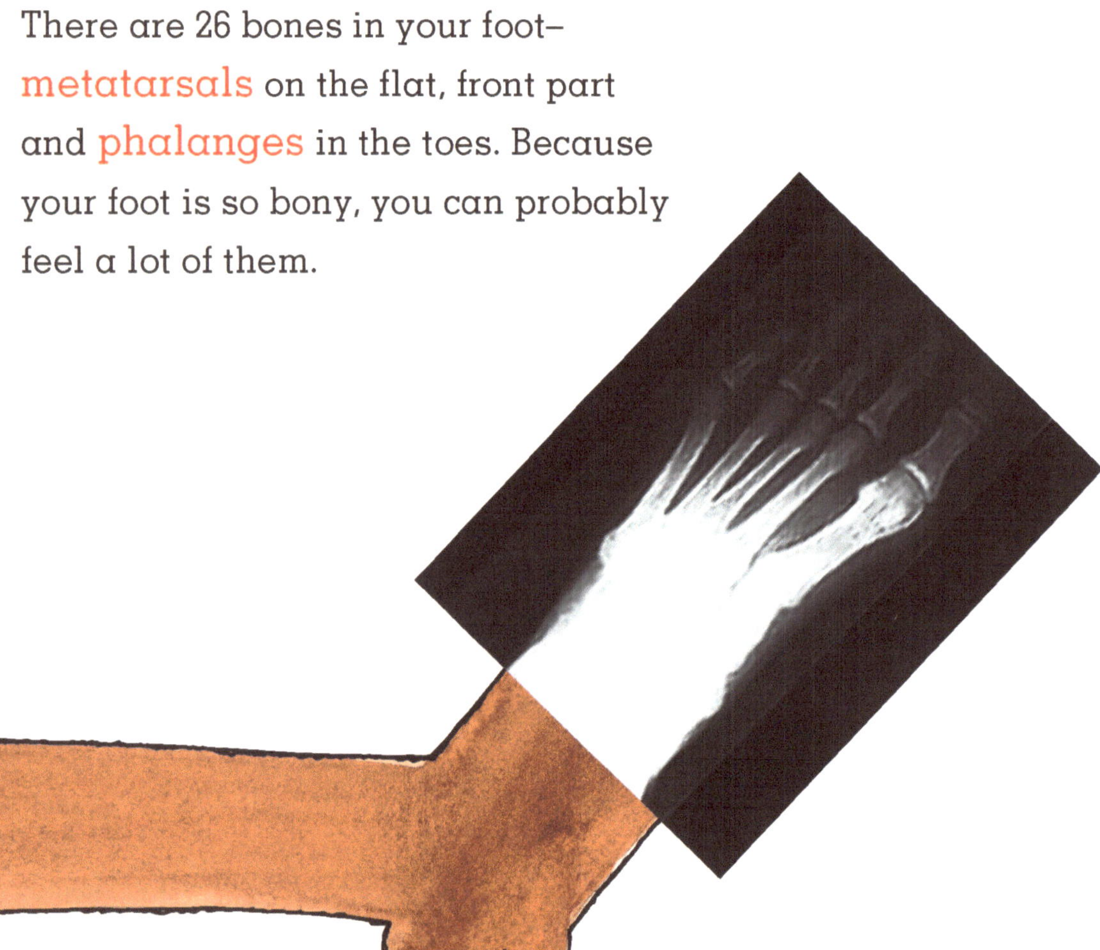

to the toe bones.

Wiggle those toes.

Do you see your phalanges move?

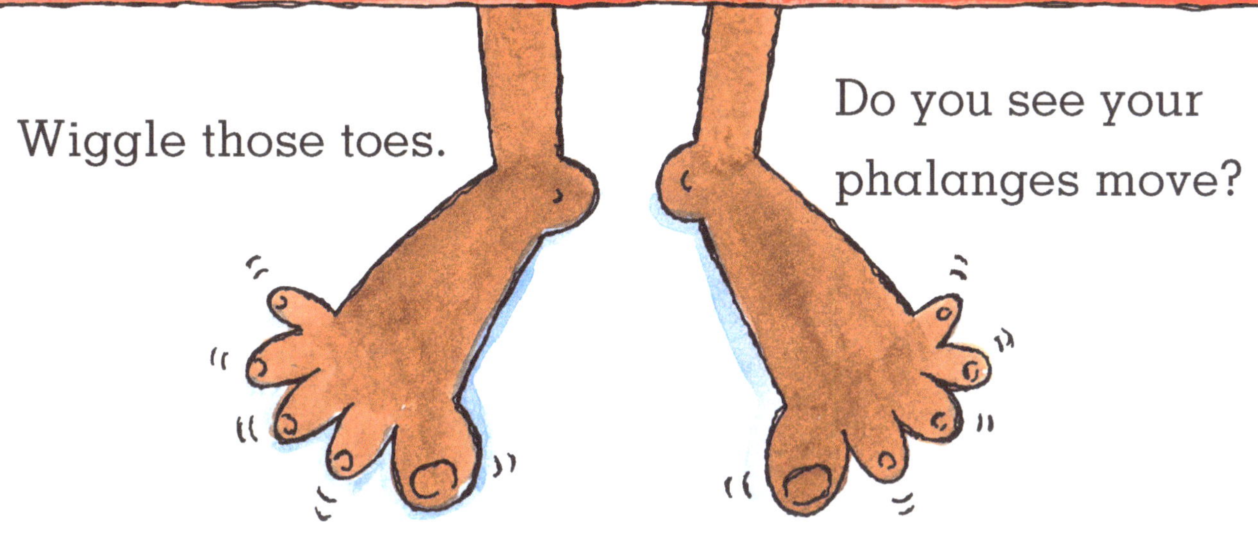

Run your hand over the top of your foot.
Do you feel the five metatarsals—one from each toe?

The arm bones are connected

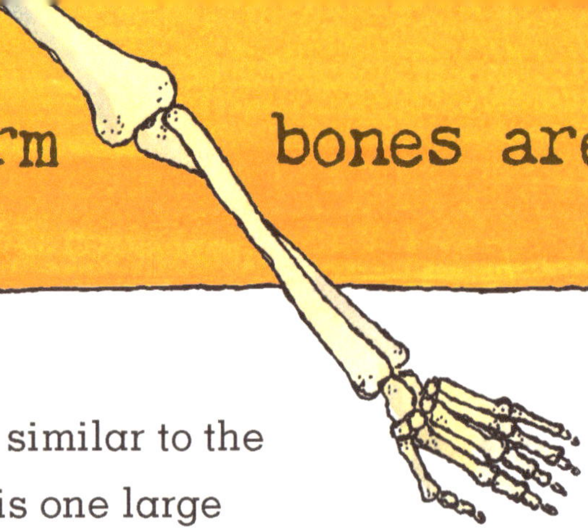

The arm is similar to the leg. There is one large bone in the upper arm, the humerus, which ends in the "funny bone." As you probably know, it's not at all funny when you bump this bone. That's because you are hitting the nerve that runs along it.

Ouch!

There are two bones in the lower arm, the radius and the ulna. Try to feel both of them. The radius is easy; the ulna is more difficult because it's the smaller of the two.

to the wrist bones.

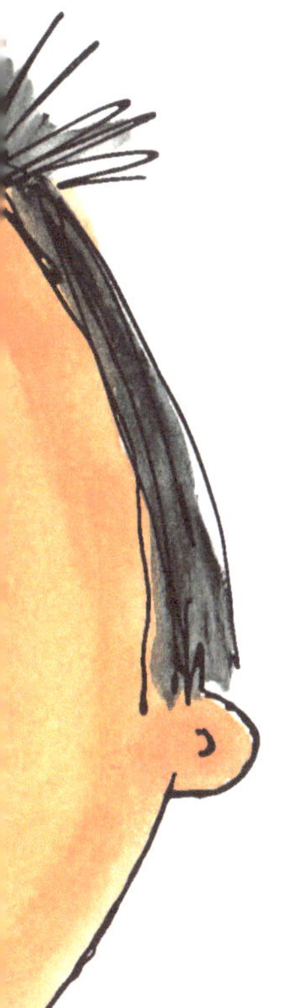

The wrist bones are connected to the hand bones, and the hand bones are connected to the finger bones!

There are 27 bones in your hand—metacarpals on the flat, front part and phalanges in the fingers. Because your hand is quite bony, you can feel a lot of them.

Bend those fingers. Do you see your phalanges move? (Make sure you bend at every joint.)

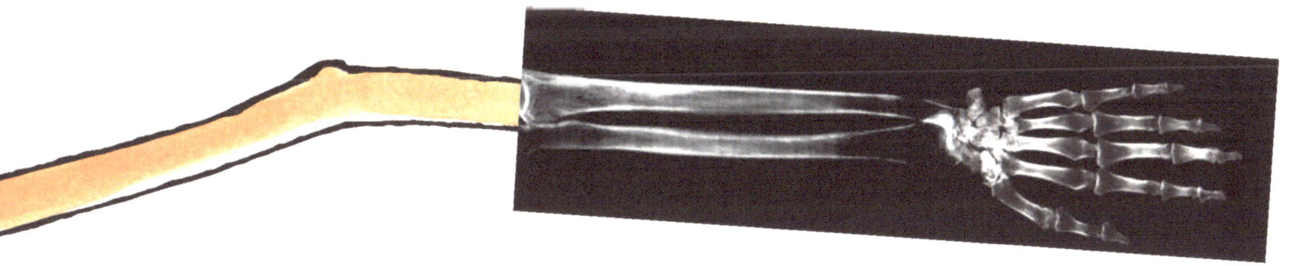

Run the fingers of your left hand over the top of your right hand. Do you feel the five metacarpals—one from each finger?

There are eight bones in the wrist, among which are the "capitate," "hamate," and "trapezoid."

You can't see your bones with binoculars.

No... you can't see your bones with binoculars, but if you are injured, a doctor can see your bones after X-rays are taken. A bad fall or an accident can cause any of your bones to break. The area around the broken bone becomes swollen and painful.

Your bones are made of living cells, just like every other part of your body (except your hair and nails). When you break a bone, a blood clot soon forms around the two broken ends of the bone. A process begins whereby the bone cells start making new bone.

A body's repair cells will make new bone and knit together a broken bone without any help from a doctor. But unless the bone is set in exactly the same position (usually with a cast) and then kept that way for a while, the bone may not heal properly. A person may end up with one arm shorter than the other, or a crooked leg.

With the help of X-rays, the doctor can set the broken bone in exactly the right position. Later, another set of X-rays will show the doctor when the two ends of the broken bone are mended. Then the cast can be removed.

Dem Bones

z z z z
cranium
vertebrae
clavicle
scapula
rib cage
humerus
pelvis
radius
ulna
carpals
metacarpals
phalanges
femur
patella
tibia
fibula
tarsals
metatarsals
phalanges

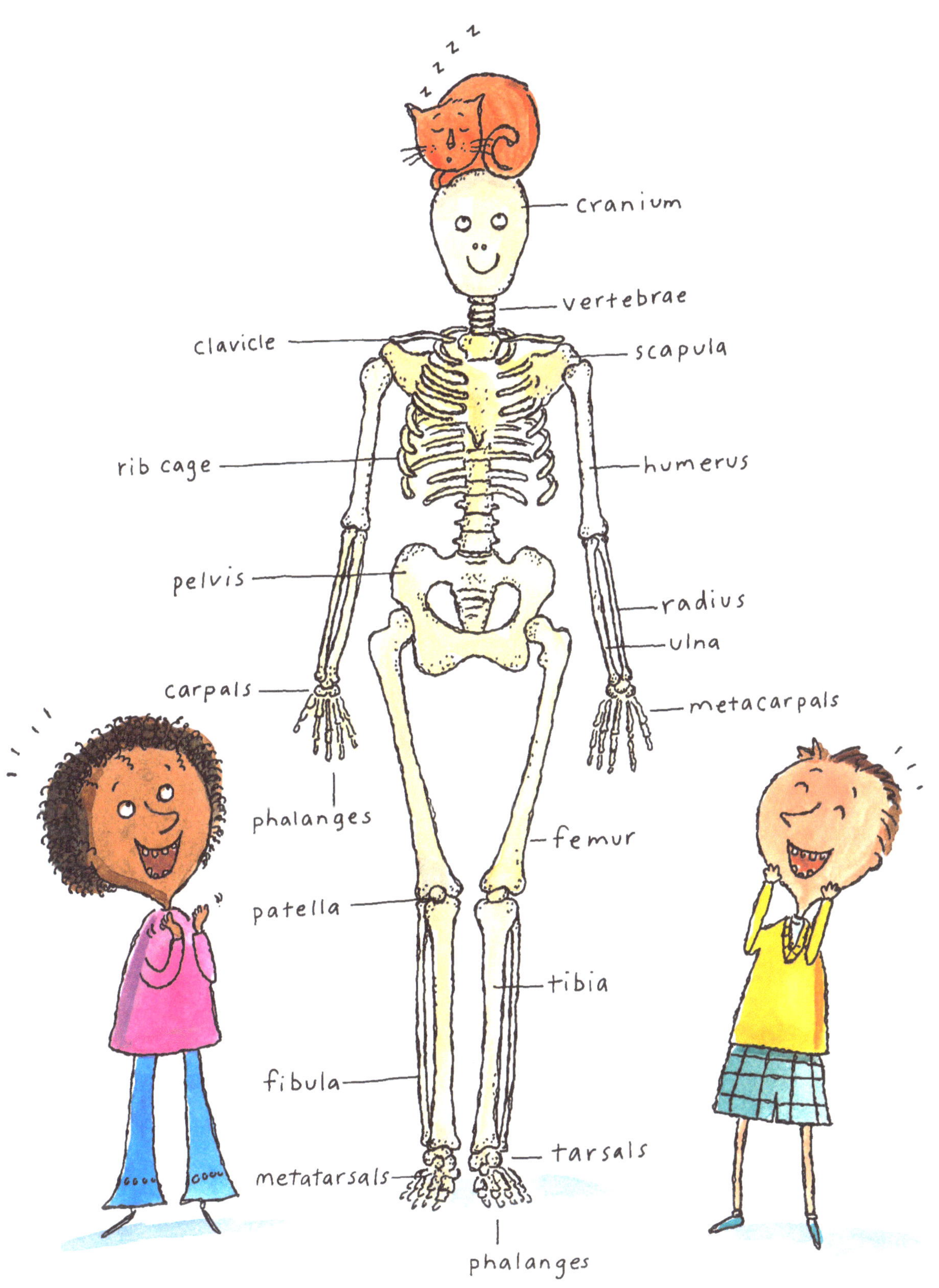

www.ingramcontent.com/pod-product-compliance
Ingram Content Group UK Ltd.
Pitfield, Milton Keynes, MK11 3LW, UK
UKHW060117300726
14090UKWH00002B/233

* 9 7 9 8 5 1 6 8 8 6 8 3 6 *